UNDERSTANDING
SCIENTOLOGY

BY CYNTHIA KENNEDY HENZEL

CONTENT CONSULTANT

Susan Setta

Associate Professor of Philosophy and Religion
Northeastern University

Essential Library

An Imprint of Abdo Publishing | abdopublishing.com

UNDERSTANDING
WORLD RELIGIONS
AND BELIEFS

ABDOPUBLISHING.COM

Published by Abdo Publishing, a division of ABDO, PO Box 398166, Minneapolis, Minnesota 55439. Copyright © 2019 by Abdo Consulting Group, Inc. International copyrights reserved in all countries. No part of this book may be reproduced in any form without written permission from the publisher. Essential Library™ is a trademark and logo of Abdo Publishing.

Printed in the United States of America, North Mankato, Minnesota
042018
092018

Cover Photo: Ted Soqui/Corbis News/Getty Images
Interior Photos: Gero Breloer/picture-alliance/dpa/AP Images, 4–5; Shutterstock Images, 8, 33; Red Line Editorial, 12–13; Chris Ware/Keystone Features/Hulton Archive/Getty Images, 14–15, 42, 46; Afro Newspaper/Gado/Archive Photos/Getty Images, 18–19; Andy Cross/The Denver Post/Getty Images, 22; Andrea Delbo/Shutterstock Images, 24, 40; Gilles Mingasson/Liaison/Hulton Archive/Getty Images, 26–27; Bob Wands/AP Images, 28–29; AP Images, 31; Mondadori Portfolio/Getty Images, 38–39, 51; Aaron St-Clair/Splash News/Newscom, 48–49; Michael Montfort/Michael Ochs Archives/Getty Images, 52–53, 58–59, 71; Denver Post/Getty Images, 65; Pierre Vinet/Warner Brothers/Photofest NYC, 67; Robin Donina Serne/St. Petersburg Times/PSG/Newscom, 68–69; Kathleen Flynn/St. Petersburg Times/PSG/Newscom, 75; Tom Gannam/AP Images, 77; Alex Millauer/Shutterstock Images, 79; Kilmer Media/Shutterstock Images, 80–81; Douglas R. Clifford/St. Petersburg Times/PSG/Newscom, 84; Chris Dorney/Shutterstock Images, 86; Kathy Hutchins/Shutterstock Images, 90; Tim Boyles/Getty Images News/Getty Images, 92–93; Arthur Mola/Invision/AP Images, 95, 96; Guillermo Legaria/AFP/Getty Images, 98–99

Editor: Arnold Ringstad
Series Designer: Maggie Villaume

LIBRARY OF CONGRESS CONTROL NUMBER: 2017961413

PUBLISHER'S CATALOGING-IN-PUBLICATION DATA

Name: Henzel, Cynthia Kennedy, author.
Title: Understanding Scientology / by Cynthia Kennedy Henzel.
Description: Minneapolis, Minnesota : Abdo Publishing, 2019. | Series: Understanding world religions and beliefs | Includes online resources and index.
Identifiers: ISBN 9781532114281 (lib.bdg.) | ISBN 9781532154119 (ebook)
Subjects: LCSH: Scientology--Doctrines--Juvenile literature. | Scientology--Juvenile literature. | World religions--Juvenile literature. | Religious belief--Juvenile literature.
Classification: DDC 299.936--dc23

CONTENTS

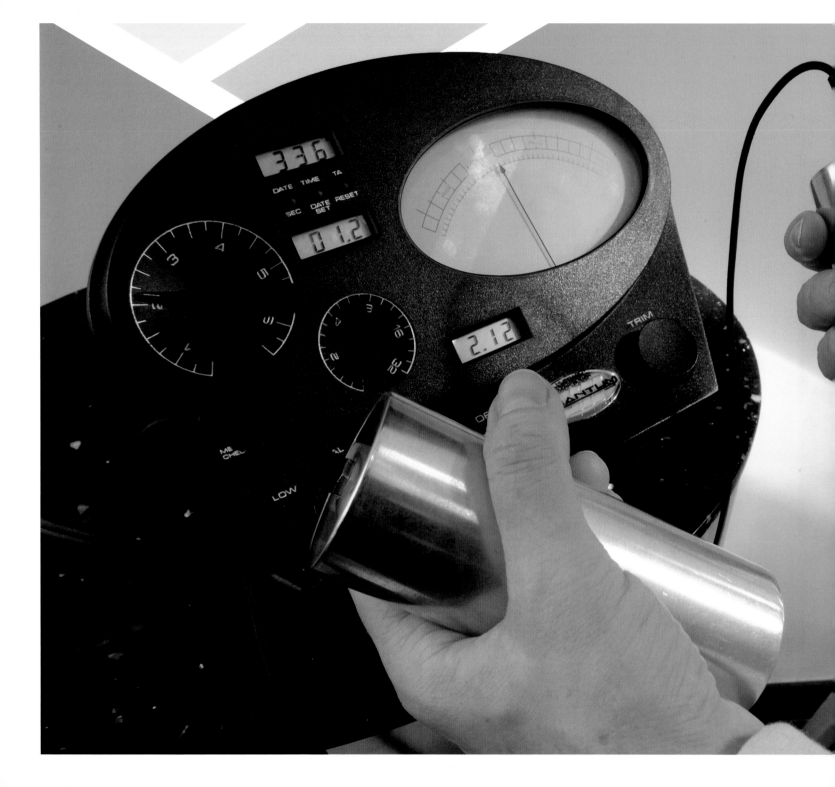

GOING CLEAR

Claire sat across the desk from her auditor, the personal counselor who would guide her through this newest session of the Scientology pathway. The pathway, known as the Bridge to Total Freedom, is a Scientologist's advancement through the religious doctrine of the Church of Scientology.

The auditor sat with her back to the door. Although they were in a huge church building, Claire couldn't hear a sound from beyond the auditing room. On the desk were the auditor's notes, shielded from Claire's view, and an E-meter.

The E-meter is an electrical device used by Scientologists in the process of auditing, or counseling. An E-meter is about the size of a large book. Following the auditor's directions, Claire picked up the E-meter's metal probes and held them, one in each hand, like bicycle grips. A readout from the E-meter would let the auditor know how

A device called an E-meter is central to the practice of auditing in Scientology.

Claire was doing, providing feedback as to how the auditor should steer the session. As Claire gently squeezed, the auditor set the sensitivity of the meter.

NEW WORDS

L. Ron Hubbard, the founder of Scientology, created a new vocabulary to explain the concepts involved in the religion. He named his program relating to mental health and personal growth *Dianetics*, from the Greek words *dia* meaning "through" and *nous* meaning "mind" or "soul." Together, they are defined as "what the soul is doing to the body."

The word *Scientology* comes from the Latin word *scio*, which means "knowing, in the fullest sense of the word," and the Greek word *logos*, which means "study of." The word *Scientology* therefore means "knowing how to know."

Starting Young

Claire was familiar with the auditing procedure and the special vocabulary of Scientology. Her parents were Scientologists. She had started out on the Scientology path at 8 years old by signing a billion-year contract with the Church of Scientology to become a member of an elite order called the Sea Org. She had also, at age 12, taken the Oxford Capacity Analysis, a personality test devised for Scientology. The test is used to interest people in Scientology by identifying areas within an individual that might be improved.

In Scientology, the concept of the reactive mind is important. This is the unconscious mind, in which scars of past traumatic incidents or losses are stored as unconscious images. These images are called engrams. A major goal of Scientologists is to suppress the reactive mind so that the active, or rational, mind can make better decisions. This allows a person's true personality to unfold. To successfully rid the reactive mind of engrams is to go Clear.

Now, after years of study, Claire was approaching Clear. She was eager to reach this state. Her life would change dramatically—or at least she believed it would.

"Take a deep breath, hold it for a moment, and let it out through your mouth," said the auditor. This produced a fall of the needle on the E-meter. The auditor interpreted this to mean that Claire was well fed and rested. Then the session began with standard questions.

"Do you have an ARC break?" That meant, "Are you upset about something?" "Do you have

OXFORD CAPACITY ANALYSIS

The Oxford Capacity Analysis, the personality test used by Scientology, is a list of 200 questions that should be answered "yes," "no," or "uncertain." Examples of questions are:

- ⊙ "Do you speak slowly?"

- ⊙ "Do you find it hard to get started on a task that needs to be done?"

- ⊙ "Do you bite your fingernails or chew the end of your pencil?"

- ⊙ "Would you 'buy on credit' with the hope that you can keep up the payments?"

- ⊙ "Is your life a constant struggle for survival?"[1]

Once the questions are answered, a personality test evaluation plots the responses above or below a line indicating the person's strengths and weaknesses. A Scientologist then goes through the results with the test taker and points out materials that might be of help.

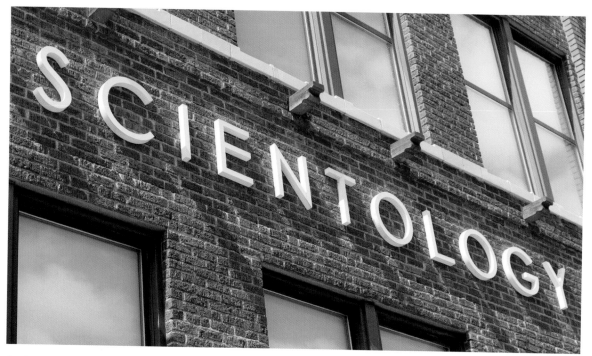
Auditing sessions take place at Scientology facilities all around the world.

a present time problem?" That meant, "Is something distracting you?" "Has a withhold been missed?" That meant, "Are you keeping something secret?"[2] The auditor monitored the E-meter as Claire answered these questions. If the E-meter needle fluctuated, the auditor identified and narrowed down the question that caused the fluctuation.

Going Deeper

Next the auditor said, "Name a time when you felt something was really real." Claire recalled an incident from her past. "Name a time when you felt something was really real," the auditor repeated.

VISITING A CHURCH

Scientology churches have many things that one would expect to find in any church. There are Sunday services held in the chapel that are open to everyone. There are services for weddings, naming ceremonies, and funerals. Churches may offer meeting space for community projects or lectures. There may be offices that coordinate community service programs.

The churches also have features that are specific to the religion of Scientology. They offer information booths, free reading materials, and bookstores so people can learn more about Scientology. They contain auditing rooms where those working their way up the Bridge to Total Freedom can audit using the Scientology technology. And there are Friday night graduations to celebrate the members' achievements of auditing or training from the previous week.

In addition, people can get free testing to identify how Scientology might benefit them. Classes offer course work in various subjects that might be helpful for students on the Bridge or people in their everyday lives. In screening rooms, people can watch technical training films and other materials. Every church has an empty office set aside for L. Ron Hubbard, the religion's founder who died in 1986, if he should need it in the future.

The auditor asked the question again and again. Each time, Claire thought of a new thing. After 30 or 40 answers, the E-meter needle floated, indicating to the auditor that Claire had overcome a trauma.

At the end of an auditing session, some Scientologists feel that talking through issues that bothered them has helped them put those issues behind them. When Claire was asked to "recall a

WORSHIP IN SCIENTOLOGY

Unlike in many other religions, there is relatively little time set aside for required worship in Scientology. Scientology churches hold religious services on Sundays, but these are not tied to any specific religious practice. Instead, many Scientologists simply like the familiarity of a Sunday service if they were brought up in another religion. Most Scientologists come to Scientology churches throughout the week at various times to participate in classes, counseling, and socializing.

time when [she was] in good communication with someone," she thought of conversations with her grandmother. After that session, she felt happy. Other times she felt the sessions were repetitive, but she continued her efforts in Scientology in the hope of climbing the Bridge to Total Freedom.

After spending hundreds of hours in classes and paying thousands of dollars, Claire went Clear in 1992. Claire was not unusual. Scientologists spend years working their way up the Bridge. Some spend hundreds of thousands of dollars in auditing fees and study materials along the way.

Claire eventually rose to the top ranks of the Scientology organization. She married a fellow Scientologist, Marc Headley. Scientology ran through every part of her life.

Finding the Truth

Scientology is extremely controversial as a religion, a community organization, and a business. Thousands of people have left Scientology, some to become vocal critics of the organization. Others have remained loyal to the religion, convinced that Scientology is the only way they can find true happiness, as well as the only way to save the planet from the destructive forces of mankind.

Scientology was founded as a religion in 1954, and it has become one of the most notable religions founded in the 1900s. It is based on the research and writings of L. Ron Hubbard, who lived from 1911 to 1986. Throughout his life, Hubbard wrote hundreds of documents and articles outlining the beliefs and practices—what Scientologists call the

ACTOR MICHAEL PEÑA

Michael Peña is an American actor. He launched his career in 1996 with a part in the movie *To Sir, with Love II* and moved to Los Angeles, California, shortly afterward. He has acted on television and in award-winning movies. He has been married to screenwriter Brie Shaffer since 2006, and they have one child. Peña and his wife are both Scientologists.

Peña was doing well after his move to Los Angeles, but he wasn't really happy. He heard actor Jenna Elfman speaking about Scientology on television. He was impressed with the idea that "Scientology enables you to be the real you without all that other stuff."[3]

Peña began practicing Scientology in 2000. He took the Purification Rundown, a Scientology program designed to help people quit alcohol and drugs, because he felt he was drinking too much. He then used Study Technology, a teaching method devised by L. Ron Hubbard, to help him improve his reading. He credits the program with helping him read scripts better, thus making him a better actor.

Peña knows that Scientology is controversial, but he is glad he joined. He ignores or dismisses the stories from ex-Scientologists as tabloid news. Peña says, "For me, [Scientology] isn't religion like a belief; it's practical things you do."[4]

technology—of Scientology. These are the source material for the church's teachings.

Scientology is a worldwide movement, although the status of the organization as a religion is questioned in many places. From the beginning, Scientology has been an insular and secretive religion. Unlike most religions, the rites of the church, known as Standard Technology, have been a closely guarded secret. The writings of Hubbard are copyrighted by the church.

During its existence, Scientology has been perceived as a psychiatric breakthrough, a social movement, a vicious and controlling cult, a money scam, and the only way to save humanity. Scientology's legal battles have been almost as famous as the celebrities that promote the religion today. More than 65 years after its founding, many people still question what exactly Scientology is.

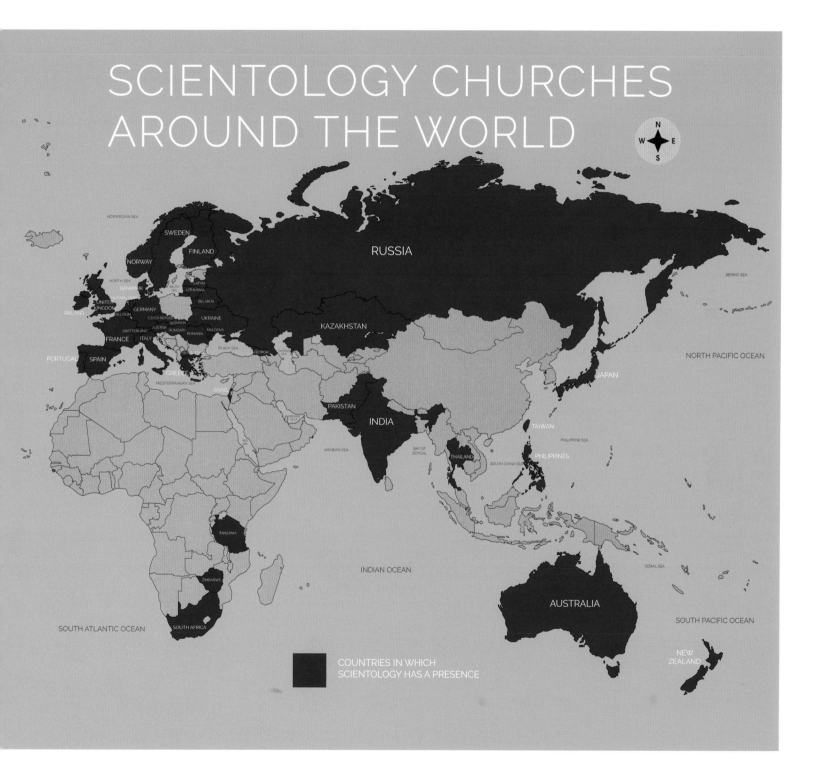

SCIENTOLOGY CHURCHES AROUND THE WORLD

COUNTRIES IN WHICH
SCIENTOLOGY HAS A PRESENCE

L. RON HUBBARD AND DIANETICS

Lafayette Ronald Hubbard was born in 1911 in Nebraska. His family moved to Montana to be near his grandparents when he was young. Soon after, his father, a US Navy officer, was deployed during World War I (1914–1918).

After the war, the family was reunited and traveled with Hubbard's father to various US military bases. They spent time in San Diego, California; Seattle, Washington; and then Washington, DC. Hubbard joined the Boy Scouts and achieved the rank of Eagle Scout soon after his thirteenth birthday. During this period, young Ron met Commander Joseph Thompson, a US Navy psychoanalyst and medic. According to the official Scientology biography of Hubbard, this encounter launched his interest in the study of the mind.

L. Ron Hubbard spent much of his life writing about and spreading Scientology.

Back in Washington State, Hubbard went to high school while his father was stationed on the Pacific island of Guam in 1927. During the next few years, Hubbard took several trips to China, the Philippines, and other parts of Asia and the South Pacific. Scientology histories claim that "[Hubbard] was one of the few Americans of the age to gain entrance into fabled Tibetan lamaseries" and that he "studied with royal magicians descended from the court of Kublai Khan."[1] Hubbard's diaries of the time do not mention these encounters.

Hubbard spent his spare time writing short stories and essays. He studied for the Naval Academy exam, failed it once, and then was dismissed because of his nearsightedness. He went back to Washington, DC, to prepare for entrance exams to George Washington University.

Hubbard got into the university, enrolling in 1930. He majored in civil engineering. During time off from school, he continued to engage with his two loves—adventure and stories. He got a license to fly a glider. Official Scientology biographies expand on this, saying he was "a barnstorming aviator through the 1930s."[2] An expedition he organized to the Caribbean to search for pirate treasure ended when the captain turned the boat around and returned to port. Later, Hubbard claimed to have placed treasures the expedition found in museums and said he had given the photographs to the *New York Times*. There is no record of this.

Back at George Washington University, Hubbard was a poor student. He often missed classes and earned poor grades. He was put on probation, and then he dropped out of school in 1932.

Becoming a Writer

Needing to make money, Hubbard started doing what he did best—telling stories. He became a pulp fiction writer, eventually specializing in science fiction and fantasy. He was a prolific writer, at times averaging 75,000 to 100,000 words a month, and he wrote under several pen names.

With a steady income, Hubbard married fellow glider enthusiast Margaret (Polly) Grubb in 1933. They had two children, L. Ron Hubbard Jr. and Katherine. In 1936, they moved to Bremerton, Washington, to be near family, but Hubbard was often away in New York to be near his publishers and fellow writers.

An event in 1938 changed Hubbard's life. He was having dental work done under anesthesia. When he woke up, he had a memory of having died and then been brought back to life. While he was dead, he remembered going through large gates and having the secrets of the universe

CLASSIC PULP FICTION

Two of L. Ron Hubbard's pulp-fiction books, *Fear* (1940) and *Final Blackout* (1940), are considered classics in the genre of pulp fiction. *Fear* is the horror fantasy tale of an ethnology professor who doesn't believe in demons or other superstitions. Then he realizes he can't account for four hours of time. As he tries to figure out what has happened, he is warned that to find the four hours means to die. *Final Blackout* is often considered Hubbard's best work of science fiction. It is a dystopian novel that calls for the need of extraordinary individuals to save a future world, a theme carried forward in Scientology.

Hubbard served aboard a submarine chaser during World War II.

revealed. Then he was pulled back to life. This near-death experience had a profound effect. He wrote the details in a manuscript called *Excalibur*. The manuscript was never published and the contents remain a secret, but from the experience Hubbard is said to have come up with one word to describe the human quest—"Survive!"

More Adventures

Hubbard joined the US Naval Reserve in 1941, months before the United States entered World War II (1939–1945). According to official records, his naval career was not noteworthy. Late in the war, he complained of stomach pain and was hospitalized for several months. Hubbard was discharged in

NAVAL CAREER

Hubbard originally trained as a naval intelligence officer. However, on his first two commands he was dismissed as "not satisfactory for independent duty" and "not temperamentally fitted for independent command."[3] He was sent to submarine-chaser school. On his first command, he claimed to find a submarine, and his ship spent hours shooting at it and exploding depth charges. No submarine was ever identified, and the ship was ordered back to port. Later, near San Diego, his ship carried out target practice by shelling South Coronado Island, which Hubbard did not realize belonged to Mexico. He was relieved of command for firing on an ally.

1946 due to ulcers. Rather than rejoin his family, he moved into a house owned by engineer John Parsons and became involved in hypnosis, magic, and the occult.

Hubbard, with his red hair and large lips, was a striking figure. He was extremely charismatic and kept audiences mesmerized with stories of his exploits. Although many people may have doubted the strict truth of some of his stories—one listener estimated that for Hubbard to do everything he had claimed, he must be 483 years old—he could hold an audience with his tales of adventure.

Hubbard's time with Parsons was short lived. He and Parsons's girlfriend, Sara Northrup, hatched a plan to buy and sell yachts using mostly Parsons's money. They flew to Florida and took off on one of the yachts. Parsons, thinking he was being scammed, put an end to their plans. In 1946, Hubbard married Northrup, though Hubbard had not divorced his first wife.

The Breakthrough

Hubbard continued writing and developing the theory that would become the foundation for Scientology. He theorized that the human mind has two parts. The analytical mind is accurate, rational, and logical. This is the conscious mind. The other part of the mind is the reactive mind. This part of the mind stores memory traces, especially those dealing with pain or trauma, from past experiences. People are not normally aware of these memory traces.

The reactive mind stores these past experiences of pain and trauma as engrams, complete images of past experiences. Engrams, Hubbard theorized, were the cause of neurosis, physical illness, and even insanity. Engrams kept the analytical mind from performing at its highest level.

Hubbard's breakthrough was the discovery of a method to identify a person's engrams and eliminate them. An engram might be a paranoia like fear of the dark. It might be a feeling of depression from a great loss. Or it might be the inability to stand up to others or maintain one's self-respect.

Auditing

The process, or technology, of identifying and eliminating engrams was called auditing. Auditing entailed questioning by an auditor, a person trained to ask the appropriate questions under Hubbard's method. The auditor's goal was to help a person identify an engram. The person then relived the

Photos of L. Ron Hubbard can be found in Scientology offices across the globe.

THE E-METER

E-meter is short for *electropsychometer*. The device measures electrical resistance in the skin. Famous Swiss psychiatrist Carl Jung, whose work centered on the unconscious mind, had measured changes in how the skin conducts electricity in response to emotionally charged words by 1906. There is little modern scientific support for the notion that measuring electrical resistance can provide any meaningful information about the person being tested.

The E-meter was invented by Volney Mathison in 1940. He worked with Hubbard in the early 1950s. Hubbard broke with Mathison in 1954 and created the Hubbard E-meter. He claimed that the new meter was so sensitive that it could detect a "tomato's scream when sliced."[4] The Hubbard E-meter has been modified over the years, but the basic structure remains the same.

experience that had created the engram and related experiences until they could eliminate the engram. It was like doing something again and again until the act was automatic, only in this case, the experience that caused the engram was revisited until it lost power over the individual.

Once all engrams were eliminated, a person became Clear. This was a state of high performance in which a person's true personality could develop, free from the inhibiting weight of engrams. A Clear could work at the highest levels, becoming more intelligent and healthier. Those who were Clear became their best selves.

Large celebrations are held when Scientology opens up new locations around the globe, including this one in Milan, Italy. These new centers continue to teach and spread the concepts of Dianetics and auditing.

To aid auditors in identifying engrams, Hubbard used the E-meter. The E-meter was a small black box with dials and knobs attached by wire to two cylinders. The original models used empty tomato soup cans for the cylinders. The E-meter measured the passage of electricity through the skin. Auditors were trained to watch the dial of the E-meter for signs of stress from a preclear, someone who was not yet Clear. The E-meter helped the auditor identify engrams and allowed the auditor to know when an engram had been cleared. Hubbard called his new therapy Dianetics.

In May 1950, *Astounding Science Fiction* published "Dianetics: The Evolution of a Science" as a nonfiction article. Later that year, *Dianetics: The Modern Science of Mental Health* was published as a book. In it, Hubbard dismissed modern theories of psychiatry in favor of using the mind to heal itself.

CHAPTER THREE

FROM SCIENCE TO RELIGION

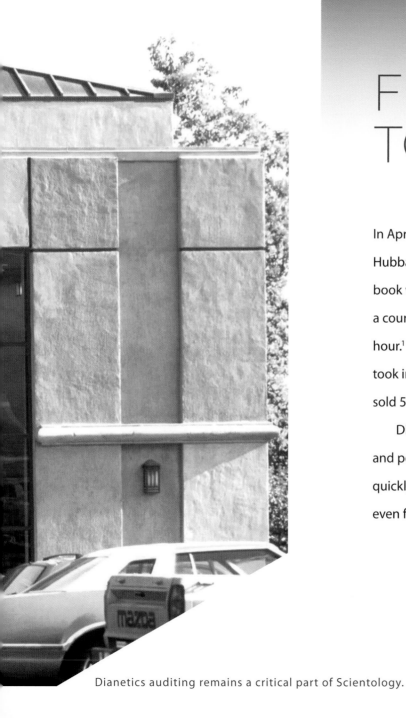

In April 1950, before the highly anticipated release of *Dianetics*, Hubbard set up the Hubbard Dianetics Research Foundation. The book was an instant hit when it came out in May. People could take a course and become an auditor for $500. Auditors charged $25 an hour.[1] Intensive ten-day audits cost $600 to $1,000.[2] The foundation took in $1 million in its first year. By the end of 1950, Hubbard had sold 500,000 copies of *Dianetics*.[3]

Dianetics auditing businesses popped up around the country, and people started informal groups to audit each other. Auditing quickly became popular. It was seen as new, interesting, and even fun.

Dianetics auditing remains a critical part of Scientology.

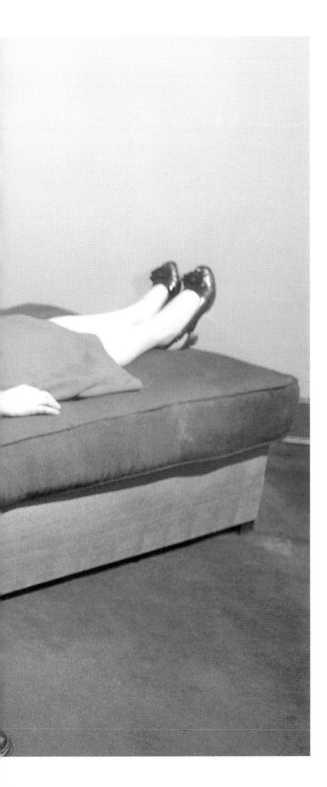

Hubbard was disdainful of the practices of mainstream psychiatry.

Mental Health in the 1950s

To understand the phenomenal success of Dianetics, it is important to put Hubbard's ideas into historical context. Mental health was a huge issue during the 1950s. Following the intense trauma of World War II, veterans' hospitals housed tens of thousands of veterans dealing with psychiatric issues. Other mental institutions housed 500,000 patients by the early 1950s. By the mid-1950s, there were more people being treated in hospitals for psychiatric problems than for any other type of disease. Yet there were only about 600 psychoanalysts in the entire United States.[4]

Treatment of mental health issues was expensive and at times harsh compared with today's standards. Psychiatrists were experimenting with lobotomies, operations to remove small pieces of the brain. Electric shock treatments were used to cure mental disorders. The alternative was incarceration in a mental institution. Hubbard instead offered something people could do to improve their mental health for the price of a book, and he argued that its basis was scientific. He declared that because "Dianetics is a science, as such it has no opinion about religion, for sciences are based on natural laws, not on opinions."[5]

Psychiatry Fights Back

The psychiatric industry was not a supporter of Dianetics. Hubbard showed disdain for the methods of psychologists and warned people of the dangers of psychiatric drugs. This disdain for psychiatry increased through the years, and to this day Scientology is known for its clashes with the psychiatric industry. In a letter to his third wife, Mary Sue, in 1969, Hubbard declared it was his mission "to take over absolutely the field of mental healing on this planet in all forms."[6]

When the Hubbard Dianetics Research Foundation began to make claims that auditing could cure not only mental illness but also many physical ailments, ranging from colds and heart disease to nearsightedness, Dianetics came to the attention of the American Medical Association (AMA). Some of Hubbard's followers were arrested for practicing medicine without a license.

The US Food and Drug Administration (FDA) began questioning the use of the E-meter as a medical device. There was no independent evidence that the E-meter worked to alleviate mental illness or anything else. The FDA had not tested the meter or approved it for any medical purpose.

Where Are the Clears?

In the first few months after the release of *Dianetics*, no one had yet been declared Clear. Clears were supposed to have exceptional observational skills and memory. They worked at a higher level than normal people. But there was no one to point to as an example.

Hubbard declared his first Clear, Sonia Bianca, in 1950. To showcase the exceptional abilities and memory of a Clear, Hubbard arranged a demonstration in Los Angeles, California, before 6,000 people. But the nervous student could not even

Hubbard spoke at the first national meeting of Dianetics auditors in 1951.

remember simple facts like the color of Hubbard's tie that she had seen moments before. It was a fiasco.

Although Hubbard was a good promoter, he was a poor manager. The money went out as fast as it came in. By 1952, he was bankrupt and forced to sell what remained of the Hubbard Dianetics Research Foundation for $6,000 to a friend and business partner in Wichita, Kansas.[7]

The New Spirit

As he had done many times before, Hubbard recreated himself. After marrying Mary Sue in 1952, he moved to Phoenix, Arizona. He set up a new organization at what is today known as the Camelback House, near the current Church of Scientology of Phoenix. It was at this time that Dianetics moved past being a set of self-help techniques and became a religion.

Hubbard had noted that during auditing sessions, people had reported engrams that had occurred while they were in the womb. Some had even reported engrams formed before they were conceived. They recalled images from past lives. At first Hubbard was skeptical.

But then he began exploring engrams formed in past lives. This lost the support of many who were fans of his science of mental health but felt the idea of reincarnation was nonsense. For others, though, the investigation of past lives was intriguing.

Dianetics has been translated into many languages and is still sold across the world.

BRAINWASHING

Opponents of Scientology claimed that auditing was a form of hypnosis or brainwashing. Interest in brainwashing began in the 1950s when the United States suspected that China and North Korea used methods such as isolation and sleep deprivation to alter the minds of American prisoners of war so that they would renounce their country. The term was also applied to cults that were said to use isolation from family and friends, along with repetitive chanting, to alter the minds of recruits.

Psychologists today consider brainwashing to be just another method of influencing a person's thinking, alongside other methods such as compliance, persuasion, and education. These methods are used every day by everyone from parents to advertisers to politicians in an attempt to change people's opinions. Most experts do not believe that the mind can be permanently altered by these techniques.

Thetans

A new doctrine came from Hubbard's investigations into past lives. Scientologists believe that humans are composed of three parts: the body, the mind, and the thetan. The body and mind work together within the human body. When the body dies, the mind dies. Early Dianetics addressed the mind.

By 1951, Hubbard began research into the spiritual nature of humans—the thetan— that other religions might view as the soul. Scientologists believe that the thetan is housed in the human body but is a separate entity. The thetan does not die with the body, but is instead reincarnated through time. Thetans have existed for 60 trillion years, as outlined in Hubbard's

THE EIGHT DYNAMICS

In 1956, Hubbard wrote *Scientology: The Fundamentals of Thought*, which laid out the Eight Dynamics. The first four Dynamics Hubbard had identified in his development of Dianetics. First was Self. This is the urge to survive as an individual in the body and the mind for as long as possible. Next was Creativity. This is the urge to make things for the future. It includes having and raising children. After that was Group Survival. This is the urge to survive as a group with other individuals. The group may be friends or a business, or it may be an entire nation. Then came Species. This is the urge to survive as a species.

The last four Dynamics Hubbard developed as part of Scientology. One was Life Forms. This is the urge to survive along with all life forms, including plants, animals, and other living things. Next was Physical Universe. This is the survival of the physical universe of matter, energy, space, and time. The seventh Dynamic was Spiritual Universe. This is the survival of a person as a spiritual being. The final Dynamic was Infinity. This is the urge toward existence as Infinity, the understanding of everything.

1952 book, *The History of Man*. By the early 1950s, auditors began exploring the past lives of thetans through auditing.

Although Dianetics and Scientology are related, they are not the same thing. Dianetics treats the physical body. The goal of Dianetics was to unleash the power of the human mind by removing the power of engrams in the reactive mind. But once a person is Clear, Scientology is meant to treat the thetan. The goal of the new religion of Scientology was to unleash the thetan's power. Dianetics was no longer simply a self-help technique, mental health therapy, or way to heal the body. It had moved into the spiritual realm.

The First Churches

The timing for this shift coincided with broader changes in American society. In the 1950s, the United States experienced a religious revival in response to the rise of Communism and the threat of nuclear annihilation during the Cold War. The archenemy of the United States was a Communist country, the Soviet Union. The Soviet government's official religious stance was atheism. Many in the United States sought to draw a distinction between the two nations by embracing religion. Popular evangelists, such as Billy Graham, drove increased church attendance. Hubbard's new melding of the science of Dianetics with the renewed interest in religion was perfect for the times.

In 1952, Hubbard started the Association of Scientologists in Phoenix. By late 1953, Hubbard had incorporated several churches. The entrepreneur had learned his lesson about allowing his new organization to grow

HUBBARD'S RECORDS

Guinness World Records notes several records held by L. Ron Hubbard. These include the most works published by one author. Hubbard published 1,084 works.[8] He also holds the records for most translated author, author with the most audiobook titles, and single most translated nonreligious work for *The Way to Happiness*, a booklet about morality.

unsupervised. Scientology grew under a new business structure. Churches were set up as franchises, with each one working as a separate business but giving a percentage of its earnings to the Association of Scientologists. Hubbard received a salary of $125 a week plus a house, a car, and travel expenses.[9] In addition, he received commissions on E-meters and teaching manuals, royalties from his books, and speaking fees.

Hubbard encouraged his new ministers to wear uniforms and conduct themselves as clergy. Scientology adopted the eight-pointed cross as its symbol, each point representing one of the Eight Dynamics. For Scientologists, these are the eight ways in which individuals strive to survive. They range from the drive for simple self-preservation to the quest for an infinite, godlike understanding of the universe. In 1954, Hubbard opened a church in California. The next year, the Church of Scientology was incorporated in Washington, DC. The church and its doctrine were rapidly expanding.

GROWTH AND EXPANSION

There were several advantages to becoming a religion. Religious practices, unlike both physical and psychological medical practices, are not regulated. Auditing, like practices and rituals from other religions, could be done with no interference from the government. The E-meter, which was once the highlight of Dianetics technology, was now termed a religious artifact used to conduct spiritual services.

Another advantage was monetary. As a church, Scientology would not have to pay taxes on its profits. Religious organizations, due to the separation of religion and government in the First Amendment to the Constitution of the United States, operate tax free. Still, Hubbard had to convince the government that Scientology was a real religion and not just a scheme to avoid taxes.

In the late 1950s, Hubbard worked to turn Dianetics into the religion of Scientology.

The Scientology symbol can be seen on many of the religion's buildings.

In the Scientology Creed, Hubbard stated "that the study of the Mind and the healing of mentally caused ills should not be alienated from religion or condoned in nonreligious fields . . . [and] that the spirit alone may save or heal the body."[1] He was not only making a case for his new religion but also dismissing the field of psychiatry for not addressing the spiritual nature of man.

A Religion?

Scientologists still came to the attention of the government. In 1958, the Washington, DC, church lost its tax-exempt status. The Internal Revenue Service (IRS) ruled that Scientology did not meet the requirements of a religion. One concern was that Scientology was involved in mental health to the point of practicing medicine without a license. The IRS also questioned the church's selling of auditing sessions and materials for a set price instead of asking for donations. This made it seem as though church funds were being used for business purposes.

Hubbard continued to make the case for Scientology as a religion. For those familiar with Hubbard's science fiction books, many of the themes of the new religion were familiar. But some elements of Scientology could be seen as rooted in other faiths. Reincarnation had similarities to the Eastern religions of Hinduism and Buddhism.

THE SCIENTOLOGY SYMBOL

The Scientology symbol is an S with two triangles. The S stands for Scientology. The lower triangle is the A-R-C triangle. The letters stand for Affinity, Reality, and Communication. Affinity is the affection or liking of something. Communication does not work without some degree of affinity. Reality is for agreement. Communication is the exchange of ideas between two people. The three factors add up to Understanding, for they are all interlinked.

The upper triangle is K-R-C. These letters stand for Knowledge, Responsibility, and Control. These three are also interrelated. Scientologists believe that as one element is improved, the other elements improve also.

Hubbard at Saint Hill Manor with, *from left*, Mary Sue, Suzette, Quentin, Diana, and Arthur

In 1954, Hubbard claimed that Scientology was closest to Hindu and Buddhist beliefs and that the earliest ancestor of Scientology was the Vedas, a body of ancient Indian texts. The illusionary nature of the universe had roots in the early teachings of the Christian Gnostics. But Hubbard's methodology of religious practice was new.

Saint Hill

By 1959, Hubbard had decided to expand internationally. He bought a mansion in England known as Saint Hill Manor. The ornate 225-year-old estate building was surrounded by approximately 55 acres (22 ha) of rolling hills.[2] Hubbard, Mary Sue, and their four young children moved to England. Saint Hill became a site for advanced auditing, and Hubbard dedicated his time to developing the new religion.

It was during his time at Saint Hill that Hubbard developed a more complete and structured theology for Scientology. One achievement during this period at Saint Hill was an early version of the Bridge to Total Freedom, which outlined the systematic path students must take to achieve mental and spiritual freedom. The Bridge requires people to train as auditors and receive auditing themselves.

BIG MONEY

Rather than collecting money from members in the ways that traditional religions do, such as through tithing, weekly donations at services, or charging for ceremonies, Scientology raises money by selling training and auditing technology to its members. The higher the level of auditing, the more expensive the donation.

Hubbard insisted that Scientology was not to be accepted on faith but was rather a way to seek knowledge. In 1961 he wrote: "Nothing in Scientology is true for you unless you have observed it and it is true according to your observation."[3]

Barriers

Hubbard recognized that a barrier for students trying to master the materials of Scientology was an inability to study effectively. In his Study Technology, he identified three barriers to effective understanding: misunderstood words, a lack of mass, and too steep a gradient.

Study Technology includes exercises to understand every word that is read instead of simply skipping over those terms the student does not understand. In practice, this means using a dictionary to look up every unknown word. The second barrier, lack of mass, means that the student does not understand the physical universe. To help students understand physical concepts, they are required to draw or create a three-dimensional model of an object. The third barrier to understanding involved students trying to learn material in the wrong sequence or before they were developmentally ready. Hubbard referred to this as being too steep a gradient. Students were often required to take Study Technology before they could move ahead to further learning. Once preclears began auditing, there was a strict advancement of steps toward becoming Clear. Preclears might advance at different speeds, but every level had to be completed.

Other barriers to advancement were overts and withholds. An overt is an act against the moral code of a group, whether the act is intentional or unintentional. In other religions, this might be called a sin. An overt might be telling a lie, hurting someone either accidentally or purposely, or breaking a rule. A withhold is hiding or not admitting to an overt.

Keeping Scientology Working

Hubbard outlined the orthodoxy, or doctrine and practices that must be followed, in a letter to his followers called "Keeping Scientology Working" (KSW). KSW insisted that all Scientologists follow Hubbard's instructions exactly. This would ensure that Hubbard remained the sole source for all materials used in the church. It also meant that these materials must remain secret so that only those authorized by the church could use them. Hubbard said, "When somebody enrolls, consider he or she has joined up for the duration of the universe—never permit an 'open-minded' approach. If they're going to quit let them quit fast. . . . Never let them be half-minded about being Scientologists."[5]

Part of Hubbard's work at Saint Hill involved experiments on plants and whether they feel emotions.

One of the most important manuscripts during the time at Saint Hill was the development of the Saint Hill Special Briefing Course, or Special Course. The Special Course was a comprehensive training course for auditors to ensure that the auditors were doing the auditing exactly as they should. The course required intense study of Hubbard's writings and took at least one to two years to complete. Graduates of this course became "Dukes of the Auditor Elite," or Class VI auditors.

Beyond Clear

Until 1966, the highest level of achievement in Scientology was to become Clear. Then Hubbard said he made more discoveries. Beyond Clear was a state of existence known as Operating Thetan (OT). As an OT, a person could have out-of-body experiences and special powers. He or she could explore the universe. However, it required auditing for the person to reach his or her full potential.

Each individual, according to Scientologists, has a thetan and extra "body thetans" (BTs). Just as the reactive mind is encumbered by engrams, thetans are encumbered by BTs that attach themselves to an individual's body and cause pain and unhappiness. These BTs must be cleansed from the body for a person's true thetan to emerge and reach its full potential. By using the Scientology technology of OT auditing, thetans can be cleared of BTs. Hubbard released OT Levels I and II in July 1966. These were the next steps for a Clear to continue up the Bridge to Total Freedom.

AFLOAT

Scientology materials were copyrighted by the church. Only as a person moved up the Bridge were new materials revealed at each new level. The close control of materials was essential to the church. The auditing materials were a significant part of church doctrine, and they were seen as potentially dangerous if they fell into the hands of those unprepared to receive them. But they were more than that. They were the monetary lifeblood of Scientology. Only through taking classes, which increased in cost as a person climbed the Bridge, could someone learn the secrets of the universe.

Hubbard became more and more concerned with security. The church's dealings with the US government and medical associations had caused him to fear that people were out to destroy him. By the early 1960s, Scientology began doing what it called Security Checks, auditing to make sure its members were loyal. The church wanted to weed out anyone who released secret information, was disloyal

Since the 1960s, Scientology has carried out part of its operations aboard ships at sea.

to the church, or criticized Hubbard. In 1959, Hubbard's own son, Ron Jr., had left the church. Hubbard declared that his son had hidden crimes that had caused him to leave.

Those who were enemies of the church were considered Fair Game. They were to be sought out and attacked by any means necessary. This might include anything from threatening them with lawsuits to digging into their personal lives for information that could be used against them.

In 1966, the church formed the Guardian's Office under Hubbard's wife, Mary Sue. The Guardian's Office was responsible for public relations, gathering intelligence, and responding to attacks and legal actions. Although the policies of Security Checks and Fair Game were officially discontinued in 1968, Scientology remained a secretive organization under the watchful eye of the Guardian's Office.

Off to Sea

Due to the controversies surrounding Scientology, Hubbard realized that he was going to have to find a new home for his religion. He spent time in the newly independent African nation of Rhodesia, which is now Zimbabwe, hoping to gain power in the country. The Prime Minister, Ian Smith, became suspicious and refused to extend his visa. Other countries were equally suspicious of the new religion.

Hubbard was deported from the United Kingdom in 1968 as an undesirable alien. Since he had not succeeded in finding a country suitable for the organization, Hubbard bought ships to house his religion. The main flagship *Royal Scotsman*, later renamed *Apollo*, became the base for Scientology. At the age of 56, Hubbard set sail with his most loyal followers.

Hubbard had once hoped for a long and illustrious naval career, and now he could fulfill this ideal as the head of his own navy. He began wearing clothes suitable to his new position, including navy-style suits with gold epaulets and braid. His new title was Commodore.

Hubbard spent time on the ship auditing himself, saying that at times he remembered places where he had buried treasure in past lives. The ship sailed to these places seeking the hidden treasure. The crew would identify a place and search it, but no treasure was ever found.

Hubbard began a new life for himself and his religion at sea.

Formation of the Sea Org

Hubbard's crew was composed of loyal Scientologists. Although many of them knew nothing about crewing a ship when they signed on, they quickly learned their new positions. The most loyal Scientologists, many of them young girls, became the Commodore's Messengers. The Messengers were responsible for seeing to every need of the leader.

NSIBLE THING TO DO."

Joining the Sea Org is promoted as a noble calling within Scientology.

Messengers delivered messages from Hubbard, learning to repeat the words verbatim so they would not be misunderstood, and carried the responses back to him. They also served Hubbard's meals, washed his clothes, and stood guard outside his door. They followed him around the ship taking notes and carrying his ashtray. Over time, the Messengers became the only people who had direct access to Hubbard on a daily basis. This gave them immense power on the ship.

FALSE MEMORIES

Scientists have demonstrated that human memory is not always accurate. People can be made to vividly remember false details of events they have witnessed, such as the color of a car at a traffic accident or childhood events that they may have heard about but didn't witness personally.

Individuals can also "remember" things that never occurred. This is an important point raised by critics of Scientology who dismiss the notion of uncovering memories from past lives. Dr. Elizabeth Loftus, a forensic psychologist, has said: "If I've learned anything from 40 years of working on these issues, just because a subject tells you that they have a detailed memory that's very vivid, that doesn't mean that it's true."[1]

The Commodore's Messengers developed into a monastic order in Scientology, the Sea Organization (Sea Org). Like young monks in other religions, their job was to serve the church. They received little or no pay. They were provided basic food and lodging, and they could take auditing at reduced cost. The dedicated Sea Org members signed billion-year contracts to prove their dedication to the church.

Discipline

Although Hubbard was often jovial and the crew enjoyed his stories of adventure and discovery, discipline was strict. Over time, even small infractions could result in severe punishment. Punishment might mean being shut in a closet for days or being shunned by the crew. Hubbard also used sleep deprivation and overboarding, throwing crew members overboard and then fishing them from the water, to ensure loyalty and strict obedience. Even young children could be severely disciplined.

Being disloyal to Hubbard or Scientology could result in being named a Suppressive Person (SP). SPs are individuals who try to suppress the survival and happiness of other people. They cause fear or distress in people's lives. SPs included journalists and psychiatrists who were critical of Scientology.

An SP might also be a friend or family member who discouraged someone from joining or remaining in Scientology. Members of Scientology were encouraged to disconnect with, or shun, SPs in their lives. This meant permanent breaks with old friends or family members who were critical of Scientology.

The Wall of Fire

The Commodore did not shirk his main duties, auditing and writing a steady stream of new material. OT Level III, known as the Wall of Fire, was released in 1968. OT III was kept strictly secret. Before being invited to do the level, Scientologists were given Security Checks and had to sign forms promising never to reveal the contents. They also had to sign waivers promising not to hold the church responsible for any trauma or damage they endured.

Hubbard claimed that the knowledge OT III contained would drive most people insane—it was only for those who prepared on the Bridge. He claimed that his efforts to uncover these secrets had almost resulted in his own death. What the public eventually learned was that OT III involved aliens, spaceships, and the creation of the universe. For followers, OT III provided an important context for the religion's teachings. For critics, it was space opera equivalent to Hubbard's earlier science fiction

THE STORY OF XENU

Details from OT III materials were released to the public during Scientology court cases. According to these materials, 4 quadrillion years ago, there was a snap, a bright light, and then darkness. Thetans were forced to create the Universe of Matter, Energy, Space, and Time (MEST) to live in, and eventually they lost the awareness of their immortality. Thetans were trapped in the MEST Universe. We think of this universe as reality, but it is an illusion.

By 75 million years ago, there was a Galactic Confederacy of 76 planets ruled by the dictator Xenu. To address the problem of overpopulation, Xenu brought billions of people to Earth, placed them in volcanoes, then detonated hydrogen bombs to kill them. The thetans of these people survived and eventually attached themselves to humans. Through Scientology, individuals can cleanse themselves of these body thetans (BTs) and release the power of their individual thetan.

writing. Hubbard continued to research and write furiously. During the next two years, he released OT Levels IV and V.

Enemies

The goal of Scientology was now to clear the planet and save humanity from self-destruction. To do this, Hubbard was going to have to defeat those trying to stop the religion. He identified groups of people, including some in government and psychiatry, who were dedicated to stopping him. He hatched elaborate schemes to foil his enemies, especially members of the psychiatric industry.

Many countries, including France and Germany, considered Scientology a cult. They brought legal cases against the organization. Some countries banned Hubbard and Scientologists, and others, such as Germany, refused to let Scientologists hold positions in parliament.

In 1973, France convicted Scientology and Hubbard (in absentia) of fraud and sentenced Hubbard to four years in prison. Hubbard set sail for the United States. He hid out in New York for ten months. It was here that he developed a grand plan to take down enemies who were making accusations against the church. Mary Sue was put in charge of implementing the plan, called Operation Snow White. She began the job of infiltrating governmental and nongovernmental agencies around the world.

WHAT IS A CULT?

Most people recognize established religions such as Islam, Christianity, and Buddhism. It is harder to identify a cult. In the 1900s, *cult* became a pejorative term due to extreme examples, such as the Peoples Temple and Heaven's Gate, that ended in mass suicides. Cults became synonymous with brainwashing and abuse. Academics often use the term *New Religion*, meaning a new spiritual movement whose teachings differ from those of established religions, instead of the word *cult*.

Over time, many organizations that were once deemed cults have become religions. Christianity was once considered a cult by Jews and Romans, Islam was called a cult by Christians, and Quakerism was called a cult by other Christians. Mormons were considered members of a cult by many people only a century ago.

LANDFALL

Once Hubbard rejoined the ship, more problems appeared. On a stop in the Canary Islands, Hubbard broke his arm in a motorcycle accident. Afraid to see a doctor, he suffered aboard the ship in excruciating pain. He remained locked in his room in agony and paranoia.

During his time at sea, Hubbard developed "rundowns," or methods for helping people deal with problems that might prevent them from success in auditing. The Purification Rundown, a course of treatment that included long times in saunas and taking vitamins, was implemented to rehabilitate drug users. The Introspection Rundown, which involved isolating an individual, was used to treat people who had had a psychotic break.

Suspecting enemies everywhere, Hubbard now cracked down on his loyal followers. In January 1974, he established the Rehabilitation Project Force (RPF). Sea Org members who broke Scientology rules

In his later years, Hubbard spent less time in public and focused on his work within Scientology.

L. RON HUBBARD'S FAMILY

L. Ron Hubbard was married three times and had seven children. He had two children by his first wife, Margaret Louise (Polly) Grubb. They were L. Ron Hubbard Jr. and Katherine. L. Ron Jr. left the church in 1959 and changed his name to Ronald DeWolf.

Hubbard married his second wife, Sara Northrup Hubbard, before he was divorced from Polly. They had one daughter, Alexis, who became estranged from her father. Hubbard's third wife was Mary Sue Hubbard. They had four children. The oldest, Diana, was the only one of his children who remained in Scientology and is a member of the Sea Org. The oldest son, Quentin, was a member of the Sea Org. He committed suicide at the age of 22. Their youngest children, Suzette and Arthur, are not involved in Scientology.

would be forced to do physically demanding labor to rehabilitate themselves in the eyes of the church.

Clearwater

Hubbard was ready to leave the seas for a land base, but his enemies were everywhere. When the *Apollo* tried to return to the United States, the crew discovered law enforcement waiting at the dock because of a tax case Hubbard faced in the Hawaii courts. Escaping the ambush, they set sail into the Caribbean.

Hubbard was now 64 years old and overweight. He had smoked his entire life. In 1974, while sailing in the Caribbean, he suffered a small stroke. It was time to find a home base.

Hubbard sent out scouts to locate a place to build the new Scientology center. They decided on the town of Clearwater, a retirement community on the west coast of Florida. The Church of

Scientology did not have a good reputation. Afraid that people would be reluctant to sell to them, the Scientologists set up a new company, the United Churches of Florida. The company purchased the old Fort Harrison Hotel and the bank across the street. Over time, it purchased and renovated other properties.

By the time the community discovered that Scientologists were buying up a central part of the town, it was too late to stop them. The religion had a new spiritual home, which it called Flag Land Base. Scientology would grow to become synonymous with Clearwater as Scientologists flocked to take advanced auditing at Flag. During the next few years, Scientology would buy more and more property to accommodate the influx of Scientologists.

Gold Base

Hubbard did not stay long in Clearwater. Always paranoid that he would be captured and imprisoned, he did not feel safe. He traveled to California and bought a resort near a small community called Gilman Hot Springs. International Base, the church's global headquarters, opened there.

In another part of the property, Hubbard operated Golden Era Productions, eventually known as Gold Base. This was a top secret property where Hubbard kept a residence. Few Scientologists even knew of its existence. At Golden Era Productions, Hubbard began to make training films for Scientology. He also attempted to break into the movie industry, hoping to make film adaptations of some of his successful books.

Operation Snow White

The Guardian's Office continued its legal battles with governments to establish religious status and kept up its efforts to punish individuals who criticized the church. Then, in 1976, two of its operatives, Michael Meisner and Gerald Wolfe, were caught breaking into government offices and copying files.

The break-in was part of Operation Snow White. Mary Sue and other members of the Guardian's Office were arrested and found guilty of domestic espionage. They had succeeded in planting more than 5,000 operatives in the IRS, the Federal Bureau of Investigation (FBI), the Department of Justice, and the AMA to spy for them and gather information.[1] They had used the stolen information to punish enemies and erase wrongdoing by Scientologists.

In 1977, the FBI conducted the largest raid at that time in history. It seized truckloads of documents and equipment from International Base. In 1979, Mary Sue and other Scientologists pleaded guilty to conspiracy. They were fined $10,000 and sentenced to five years in prison.[2] They appealed but were sent to prison in 1983.

As Operation Snow White unfolded, Hubbard went into hiding. He was never indicted for the crimes, although the government considered him an unindicted coconspirator. He returned to a ranch near Los Angeles in 1978. On February 14, 1980, he fled with longtime friend Pat Broeker and Broeker's wife, Annie. Hubbard became a recluse and was never seen in public again.

The Rise of David Miscavige

L. Ron Hubbard died in 1986. His isolation and then death left a void in the power structure of the church. This was quickly filled by David Miscavige, a dedicated Scientologist in his twenties who was head of the All Clear Unit of Messengers that controlled the church.

Miscavige was a prodigy in Scientology. His family joined the church when Miscavige was 10, hoping that Scientology would help control young David's asthma. The family moved to Saint Hill. He began auditing at Saint Hill when he was 12 and was giving Security Checks by the age of 13. At age 16, he dropped out of school and became a Messenger, rapidly working his way into Hubbard's inner circle. At Gold Base, Miscavige was the Chief Cinematographer. Hubbard then made him Action Chief, responsible for making sure all of Hubbard's commands were followed.

Miscavige began taking control of Scientology soon after Hubbard went into seclusion. He and Broeker became conduits through which the church communicated with Hubbard. He would meet

QUENTIN

At age 14, Quentin Hubbard, L. Ron and Mary Lou Hubbard's oldest son, was the first person initiated into OT III training. Quentin, however, was more interested in airplanes than Scientology. At age 20, he attempted suicide and was put into a Scientology auditing practice called Introspection Rundown. In 1976, he was found dead in his car from carbon monoxide poisoning. His death was ruled a suicide.

with Broeker at secret locations and receive Hubbard's materials. He would then relay the information to the Sea Org. In this way, they completely controlled information within the church.

Miscavige blamed Mary Sue and the Guardian's Office for the mess the church was in after the revelation of Operation Snow White. He forced her from power. He then began driving out those who had been close to Hubbard's wife. By 1983, Miscavige had purged the church of rogue Scientologists and become head of the Religious Technology Center (RTC), which oversaw the church's religious materials.

MARY SUE HUBBARD

After Mary Sue served her prison sentence, Scientology gave her a house in Los Angeles as a reward for her service to the church. She lived there until her death in 2002. In her will, she stipulated that the house could not be sold until the death of her beloved dog, Tzu. The dog lived another 11 years.

Scientologists and their children protested the FBI's treatment of their religion following the indictments of Mary Sue and others.

BATTLEFIELD EARTH

After L. Ron Hubbard went into seclusion, he returned to writing science fiction. One of the most notable of these novels was 1982's *Battlefield Earth*. The lengthy novel was about an Earth in the year 3000 that is ruled by an alien invader. The hero, Jonnie Goodboy Tyler, must lead the few remaining humans, now an endangered species, in an epic battle to save the planet and the universe. Written in the style of Hubbard's earlier pulp fiction, the novel received some popular praise as a fast-paced adventure. In 2007, Massachusetts governor and future presidential candidate Mitt Romney even named *Battlefield Earth* as one of his favorite books.

Hubbard wanted to make Hollywood movies from his novels, but he was unsuccessful. After Hubbard's death, *Battlefield Earth* was made into a movie in 2000. Actor John Travolta, a Scientologist, starred in the movie. He also coproduced and financed much of the film. The movie was a commercial and critical failure.

John Travolta starred as a villain in the film adaptation of *Battlefield Earth*.

Critic Roger Ebert explained that while the film did not seem to promote Scientology, it was a poor movie: "The film contains no evidence of Scientology or any other system of thought; it is shapeless and senseless, without a compelling plot or characters we care for in the slightest."[3]

RESTRUCTURING THE CHURCH

Many Sea Org members did not agree with Miscavige's treatment of Mary Sue or his rise to power in the Sea Org. By the mid-1980s, some of those leaving Scientology were going to court and claiming millions in damages, saying that the church had abused and defrauded them. Although many high-level members left the church in opposition to the management, they remained dedicated to Scientology. Splinter groups, independent Scientology groups, began forming in the mid-1980s. They were formed by members who believed in the teachings of L. Ron Hubbard but did not like the direction in which the church was going under Miscavige.

David Mayo, personal auditor of L. Ron Hubbard and his wife, had been in the church for 25 years. He had helped Hubbard develop some of the most advanced teachings and was considered his natural

David Miscavige's leadership of Scientology brought new controversies, both within the religion and in its contact with the outside world.

successor by some. When Miscavige created the RTC, with himself as head, to run the church, Mayo left. He said he had suffered physical abuse and humiliation.

Mayo opened the Advanced Abilities Center to carry on auditing outside the sanction of the church. The center attracted other ex-Scientologists, and Mayo was soon making money on this auditing. Mayo was harassed by the church, which sought to force him to close. When that didn't work, the church filed a lawsuit against him. Scientology claimed Mayo had stolen trade secrets and infringed on copyrights. When the church refused to disclose advanced auditing documents, Mayo won the case. However, the Advanced Abilities Center had already been forced into bankruptcy.

The New Scientology

Once in firm control, Miscavige began a restructuring and rehabilitation of Scientology. In the late 1980s, he hired a public relations firm to improve the image of the religion. The church began supporting causes like the Goodwill Games, an international sporting competition. It ran ads promoting the philosophy of Scientology.

Then, in May 1991, *Time* magazine ran a story by Richard Behar, "Scientology: The Thriving Cult of Greed and Power." The story gave a devastating view of the church and its focus on making money from its followers. Miscavige went on a popular news show to explain the church, but his presentation was not convincing. The church went on the attack. It sued *Time* and Behar for libel and defamation. The suit went all the way to the Supreme Court, but Scientology could not prove its case.

Under Miscavige, the church continued to promote itself and the life story of its founder.

Miscavige's next goal, the Religious Freedom Crusade, was more successful. He wanted to get

Scientology recognized as a religion in the United States and internationally. The church began filing

dozens of lawsuits against the government. In 1993, Scientology and the IRS settled the long-standing

feud over Scientology's status as a religion. The church paid the IRS a small fine, and the IRS agreed

to give Scientology religious status. The government forgave the $1 billion the church owed in back

taxes. In return, the church agreed not to pursue any more lawsuits. Miscavige declared, "The war is

over."[1]

SCIENTOLOGY IN RUSSIA

Russia resisted Scientology as a religion, creating a law that allowed registration of only those religions that had been in Russia for more than 15 years. The effort was overturned in 2007 by the European Convention on Human Rights (ECHR), of which Russia is a member. This was a major victory for Scientology, allowing it to continue operating in the 47 countries in which the ECHR has jurisdiction.

Miscavige used his success in the United States to further the effort to have Scientology recognized as a religion around the world. Many countries now recognize its legal standing even though government officials and the media may resist the spread of the religion. In 2009, a French court convicted the organization of fraud and fined it $800,000.[2] But Scientology is making progress on the legal front in other places. In October 2017, Mexico recognized Scientology as a religion.

Miscavige next turned to the Scientology materials. In 1996, he announced the Golden Age of Tech. He said that many of the training levels had errors that needed correcting. Once they were fixed, the church required many Scientologists to redo training, costing some people thousands of dollars. In 2007, Miscavige republished a new package of Hubbard's essential texts called *The Basics*. Next came the Golden Age of Knowledge, the full audio restoration of all 3,000 of Hubbard's lectures. With the opening of a new Church of Scientology building in Clearwater in 2013, Miscavige announced the Golden Age of Tech Phase II. This included the release of some of Hubbard's previously unpublished writings.

Community and Social Programs

Like many churches, Scientology sponsors programs that serve people in the communities in which it operates. In 1981, Scientology published Hubbard's *The Way to Happiness: A Common Sense Guide to Better Living*. The church has distributed more than 100 million copies

CLEARWATER'S CATHEDRAL

A new Flag Building in Clearwater was opened in 2013. The building spans a city block. It can accommodate thousands of people who are auditing or training. The building's floors are paved with fine Italian travertine limestone. Arched window panels are made of a luxurious stone known as honey onyx. Sixty-two life-size bronze sculptures represent the principles of Scientology.

of this nondenominational book that contains 21 steps toward a moral life.[3] It also promotes these "Scientology Commandments" in a series of videos.

Study Technology, the set of learning techniques Hubbard developed in the 1960s, has been adapted for use by public and private secular schools as a program Scientology calls Applied Scholastics. Applied Scholastics International is an independent, nondenominational organization funded by Scientology and Scientologists. Schools in the United States and other countries can use Applied Scholastics to guide their lesson plans alongside a more traditional curriculum.

Volunteer ministers, under a training program established by Hubbard in the mid-1970s, help people in need in their communities and around the world. They use principles established by Hubbard to assist in physical, mental, and spiritual issues. A permanent Volunteer Ministers Disaster Response Team was founded to come to the aid of victims of natural or man-made disasters after the terror attacks on the World Trade Center on September 11, 2001. The Response Team works with governments and other agencies to provide physical and spiritual relief to victims.

Drugs, Crime, and Human Rights

Hubbard was an advocate of living a drug-free life and developed methods he believed would help those addicted to drugs become drug free. Narconon is a Scientology organization, founded in 1966, that runs a network of drug rehabilitation centers using methods developed by Hubbard. This includes helping patients with withdrawal, detoxification, and rehabilitation. The Truth about Drugs campaign

Students in a Louisiana school use Applied Scholastics in their classroom in 2007.

disseminates information about the harmful effects of drugs. According to 2017 statistics from Scientology, more than 1,200 organizations, governments, and law enforcement agencies, as well as 10,000 schools, have used its materials.[4]

Scientology has long been involved in prison outreach. The church believes the key to prisoners' rehabilitation is self-respect. Its Criminon program uses Hubbard's *The Way to Happiness* as a foundation for instilling a simple moral code to help prisoners reform their lives.

Scientology's distrust of mainstream psychiatry extends to its community-focused programs. The church runs a group it calls the Citizens Commission on Human Rights. The organization's mission is to investigate and oppose what it sees as psychiatric violations of human rights.

Resistance to Community Programs

Scientology stands behind the independence and effectiveness of its programs. However, it has encountered resistance from communities in which it has tried to introduce them. Applied Scholastics as well as many other Scientology-sponsored organizations have been criticized by many in the public. An Illinois law requiring teachers to teach good character qualities in school brought up a debate about whether *The Way to Happiness* could be used in schools. Critics argued that the booklet's religious origins, as well as the misdeeds of the church, meant it was inappropriate for public school students.

Celebrity Scientologist Tom Cruise speaks at an event to promote Applied Scholastics in 2003.

Others have objected to public and private schools receiving government money in the form of vouchers when those schools are using Applied Scholastics. Charles Haynes, a First Amendment expert and director of the Religious Freedom Education Project, says that while the materials as he reads them are not proselytizing, they do share much of the terminology that is specific to Scientology. For many, this association with Hubbard is still a promotion of Scientology and represents support for what they consider a cult.

The methods for drug rehabilitation at Narconon have long been questioned due to a lack of independent medical research. Although Scientology claims a 70 percent success rate, there is no independent evidence that this is true.[5] In the 2010s, lawsuits filed against the Narconon Rehab Facility in Oklahoma, the flagship facility in the United States, claimed the facility had committed fraud against its patients. Many of these lawsuits ended in the facility paying out settlements rather than admitting guilt. Investigations of the facility continue.

Criminon, Scientology's prison reform program, has been used in many prisons in the United States and internationally. According to Scientology, Criminon is used in more than 2,100 prisons in 38 countries.[6] There is no independent evidence that Criminon's methods are effective. The program is especially criticized for interference with patients who are under medical psychiatric care.

Opponents see the Citizens Commission on Human Rights as a veiled lobbying group against the field of psychiatry. The organization runs a museum in Los Angeles called Psychiatry: An Industry

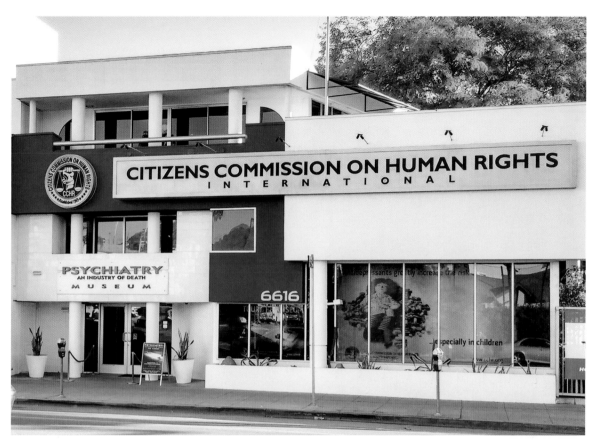

The Citizens Commission on Human Rights is headquartered in Los Angeles.

of Death. The museum's exhibits suggest not only that psychiatry is harmful to people today but also that it was responsible for World War II and the Holocaust, among other historical atrocities. Opponents claim that the organization floods news outlets with letters against psychiatric practice and has volunteer ministers who encourage people after traumatic events not to seek psychiatric help.

CELEBRITIES AND CONTROVERSIES

L. Ron Hubbard realized early in the history of Scientology that a good way to spread the word about the new religion was through celebrities. By 1955, he had started Project Celebrity to encourage Scientologists to bring celebrities into the church. Then, in the late 1960s, Scientology opened the first Celebrity Centre. These were special churches that catered to Hollywood stars and other high-profile members.

Many Hollywood stars, and those interested in making a career in Hollywood, have tried Scientology. Some, like Jerry Seinfeld and Brad Pitt, took courses or auditing in Scientology and then quit. Others, such as Leah Remini and Katie Holmes, became dedicated members before eventually leaving the church and turning into vocal opponents of Scientology.

Scientology's Celebrity Centre in Hollywood is emblematic of the church's efforts to attract high-profile individuals to the religion.

PERSPECTIVES

TOM CRUISE

When Tom Cruise became a Scientologist in 1986, he was already a world-famous actor in Hollywood blockbusters. After only seven years, he had made it to OT III, the Wall of Fire. But Cruise had a problem making the leap to the next level of Scientology.

In 1999, he became a more active member of the church. Cruise has become a monumental spokesperson for Scientology, claiming that Scientology helped cure his dyslexia. He lobbied for funding for Applied Scholastics under the education policies of President George W. Bush. He lobbied to have the US government help Scientologists gain acceptance in Germany. And he has personally given millions of dollars to the church.

Cruise has said, "I think it's a privilege to call yourself a Scientologist and it is something that you have to earn . . . because a Scientologist does. He or she has the ability to create new and better realities and improve conditions. Being a Scientologist, you look at somebody and you know absolutely that you can help them."[1]

Some people in the entertainment industry have become spokespeople for Scientology. Actor Kirstie Alley claimed that a single auditing course cured her of a cocaine addiction. Actor John Travolta, who joined in 1974 when he was 21 years old, testified that Scientology helped him overcome a fear of rejection. Perhaps the most famous public Scientologist is Tom Cruise, who has been a strong advocate for the church.

Although Cruise's outspoken support for Scientology has kept the church in the news, the media spotlight has not always been to the benefit of the church. His ex-wife Katie Holmes, once a Scientologist, divorced Cruise, citing that she did not want her daughter raised in the church. His attacks on the psychiatric field have made him the butt of jokes in pop culture.

Abuse of Power

Scientology's reputation has been tarnished by media coverage of several high-profile cases. Not only has the church's targeting of government agencies been revealed in Operation Snow White but cases against individuals have received major coverage. Journalists who have attempted to investigate Scientology have found themselves under attack by the church.

When Paulette Cooper wrote the book *The Scandal of Scientology* in 1971, she was considered Fair Game by the Church of Scientology. In what was called Operation Freakout, Cooper was followed, her telephone was tapped, she was sued 19 times, and she received death threats. The church then attempted to frame her for a terrorism charge, and she was indicted in 1973. Although she was eventually exonerated, the incident showed that people who spoke against the church would face retaliation.

Death of Lisa McPherson

Lisa McPherson joined the Church of Scientology in 1977. After many years in the church, she had not reached Clear, and she was ready to quit. But she was then put into a process called auditing repair, and by 1995 she had gone Clear.

The death of Lisa McPherson drove many people to protest the practices of Scientology.

Just three months later, in November 1995, Lisa was in a minor car accident. When paramedics arrived, they found her walking down the street naked. Paramedics tried unsuccessfully to talk to her and then took her to the hospital. The hospital wanted to get a psychiatric assessment. But when church officials arrived, they refused permission for her to be seen by a psychiatrist and took her home.

Lisa was given an Introspection Rundown. She was kept in isolation. But instead of getting calmer, she screamed and flailed. Her guards were forced to strap her down to keep her from hurting herself. She slowly deteriorated until she was not communicating, eating, or even drinking water. Although her condition became critical, those watching her did not report the problem to authorities. By the time they decided to help her, it was too late. She died on the way to the hospital.

Joan Wood, the medical examiner for the case, said that McPherson had died from a blood clot as a result of dehydration. The police launched an investigation. The church hired experts to refute Wood's findings, and she eventually declared she had changed her mind, ruling the death accidental. Authorities could not prove McPherson was murdered or died due to negligence. The case was dismissed, but it brought a lot of unwanted attention to the practices of Scientology. The McPherson family finally settled a civil case in 2004 for an undisclosed amount.

Scientology maintains a significant official web presence, where it spreads information about the religion's beliefs, practices, and achievements.

Crime and Punishment

Since the time of the *Apollo*, those who broke rules in the church were given an opportunity for rehabilitation through the RPF. Members voluntarily went to the RPF in hopes of getting back into good graces with the church. It was a way of doing penance for misdeeds. They were often assigned to hard labor rehabilitating the church's buildings.

Those who left the church often painted a dismal picture of the RPF. They reported members locked in basements, poor sanitation, barely edible food, sleeping on the floor, and working almost nonstop. They alleged that the RPF was a private prison that provided free labor for the church. This seemed to reinforce the notion that Scientology was a cult run for the benefit of a few at the top. Scientology disputes these claims.

The Internet

Scientology depended on keeping its materials secret both to protect the doctrine of the church and to generate money by selling auditing based on those materials. In the past, Scientologists have gone to great lengths to protect their interests from those who wanted to print or use the materials without permission. The internet has destroyed much of that privacy.

One of the first leaks on the internet were parts of OT III, the Xenu story. They were released onto the internet in 1994 after their use in a court case. WikiLeaks dumped large numbers of OT

SCIENTOLOGY ON THE NET

The Church of Scientology has adapted to the internet. It maintains a massive website with information on the church, the life of L. Ron Hubbard, and the many community programs run by the organization. Some of the church's internet activity has been controversial. In 2009, Scientology became the first group officially banned from posting on Wikipedia after it was caught creating accounts to delete any unfavorable information from the site.

PERSPECTIVES

KAREN SCHLESS PRESSLEY

Fashion designer Karen Schless Pressley and her husband, composer Peter Schless, moved to Los Angeles in the late 1970s. They began to meet many Scientologists and started taking self-improvement classes offered at the Celebrity Centre.

By 1986, Karen had decided to sign a billion-year contract and join the Sea Org. Karen became Commanding Officer of Celebrity Centre Network. Her job was to get more celebrities to join and spend more money on Scientology. Her husband worked at Golden Era Productions.

As Karen watched millions of dollars being poured into facilities for high-profile members, such as actor Tom Cruise, she began to believe Miscavige was abusing his power and became disenchanted. In 1991, she decided to leave. Karen was given a choice of going to RPF or being excommunicated and never seeing her husband again. She loved Peter, so she felt she had no choice. After months of hard labor in the RPF, she went back to work. But the leaders' abuse of power got worse, and she left in 1998. She never saw Peter again.

documents on its site in 2008. Although Scientology has gone to court to claim copyright on its materials, the church has found it impossible to prevent leaks. The group Anonymous, made up of internet hackers and masked protesters, has dedicated much of its time to attacking Scientology.

Ex-Scientologists

The late 1900s and early 2000s saw an exodus of many executives from the Sea Org. Many claim to have left due to disorganization at the highest levels of the church and abuse and violence at the hand of Miscavige. The church has denied the allegations. Many of the individuals who have left have written books about their experiences or maintain blogs that spread their perspectives about Scientology.

Mark Rathbun, Miscavige's Inspector General of RTC, joined the Sea Org in 1978. He left the church briefly after the 1993 IRS decision but returned in 1995. He left the church for good in 2004. Rathbun has since appeared in documentaries critical of Scientology. Mike Rinder, who became a Scientologist at age six, was the primary international spokesman for the church. He left the Sea Org in 2007, leaving his wife and two children behind. They have now disconnected from him. Actress Leah Remini told of her life in and escape from Scientology in the book *Troublemaker: Surviving Hollywood and Scientology*.

In 2011, the *New Yorker* published a story by Lawrence Wright about director and screenwriter Paul Haggis, who publicly left the church in 2009. Wright later expanded the story into a book, *Going Clear*, discussing Scientology more broadly. The book was later adapted into an HBO documentary of the same name. The book and movie have had a profoundly negative impact on many people's views of Scientology.

Claire's Story

Claire Headley went Clear by 1992. She quickly rose in the ranks of the Sea Org. Her husband, Marc, worked producing videos for the organization.

When Miscavige changed some rules on when a person had been Clear, Claire, well into her OT V auditing, was declared unclear and sent back for more Dianetics. The other change that affected Claire and Marc was a policy that those in the Sea Org were not allowed to have new children. Sea Org members worked long hours and often traveled. The church did not think having the responsibility

to care for young children allowed Sea Org members to do their jobs. The rules later changed so that anyone who was pregnant had to leave the Sea Org. They could remain Scientologists but could not keep their positions in the top ranks.

Claire and Marc had hoped to have a family, but they had dedicated their lives to Scientology as members of the Sea Org. In the next few years, Claire had two abortions. She was promoted to the elite RTC. But she was making a hard choice to give up having a family to serve her religion.

Leaving the Sea Org was not easy. If members spoke about leaving, they were given special classes to change

Actress Leah Remini is one of the most high-profile former Scientologists, and she has spoken out about her criticisms of the religion.

their minds. For those who chose to just walk out, there were rumors of what were called "blow drills." This meant doing a search for the missing person and bringing them back to the RPF. Marc finally left permanently in 2005. Not long after, he helped Claire leave. They eventually had the family they desired.

SHELLY MISCAVIGE

David Miscavige married Shelly Barnett, a loyal Sea Org member, in 1982. Shelly Miscavige worked at his side in the Church of Scientology until 2006, when she took the blame for a botched reorganization effort. Other than an escorted appearance at her father's funeral in 2007, she has not been seen in public since.

THE FUTURE OF SCIENTOLOGY

In recent years, the Church of Scientology has expanded its number of churches and other organizations. Dozens of new churches, or Scientology Ideal Organizations (Ideal Orgs), have opened throughout the world. The spiritual headquarters of Scientology, located in Clearwater, Florida, has more than 50 buildings.

There is no doubt that the Scientology infrastructure has expanded worldwide and that its legal standing has made progress. Scientology is a powerful organization. It is estimated to have amassed several billion dollars and has staff in 164 countries.[1]

Scientologists celebrated the opening of an elaborate new complex in Clearwater in 2013.

How Many Are There?

By the 1990s, the church claimed 8 million adherents.[2] More than two decades later, the Church of Scientology claimed about 10 million members worldwide. That is almost as many Scientologists as there are people of the Jewish faith, which had 14 million members worldwide as of 2012.[3] This figure would put Scientology among the major religions in the world.

But according to Lawrence Wright's 2013 book, *Going Clear*, a more realistic estimate is fewer than 50,000 members. Mike Rinder, an ex-Scientologist who runs a website opposed to the church, puts the real number at fewer than 30,000.[4] This seems more in line with statistics put out by independent agencies. According to the American Religious Identification Survey (ARIS) in the United States, people identifying as Scientologists numbered 45,000 in 1990, 55,000 in 2001, and only 25,000 in 2008.[5]

Part of the large difference in numbers may be due to how membership is counted. Scientologists

---

FREEWINDS

Just as it was in Hubbard's time, a presence at sea is an important part of Scientology today. The vessel *Freewinds* began as a Church of Scientology religious retreat in 1988. The 440-foot (130 m) boat is used for conventions and special events.[6] One such event is the annual Maiden Voyage Anniversary of the *Freewinds*, a weeklong celebration for leading Scientologists. The church also offers special courses that are available only on the *Freewinds*.

Lawrence Wright brought considerable new attention to Scientology and its practices in his 2013 book, *Going Clear.*

often count members as anyone who has purchased Scientology materials or anyone who has ever taken a Scientology course. This is very different from the number of people who identify their religion as Scientology.

Religion or Cult?

Scientology has devoted a great deal of effort and spent millions of dollars to be recognized as a legitimate religion. However, there is not always a clear distinction between what is a religion and what is a cult. Academics often prefer to use the term *New Religion* when addressing religions that have arisen in the last 100 years,

Mike Rinder spoke to the press at the premiere of the documentary film adaptation of *Going Clear.*

such as the Unification Church, Hare Krishna, and Scientology, as opposed to long-standing traditional religions like Judaism or Hinduism.

Scientology is often condemned for the methods it has used to punish individuals and organizations that criticize the church. It has lost legal battles over its persecution of individuals and its covert infiltration of government offices. Many ex-Scientologists have testified to the harassment they faced while in the church and after leaving it. Church officials deny these allegations.

At the same time, many devoted Scientologists speak highly of the church and how it has changed their lives. They staunchly defend it against its critics. And observers have noted that its belief system is in many ways no stranger than the beliefs of Christianity, Islam, or any other established religion. It is simply newer.

The beliefs of Scientologists, and their ability to practice their faith, are protected under the concept of religious freedom in the United

HOW MANY SCIENTOLOGISTS IN OTHER COUNTRIES?

Countries outside the United States report numbers of Scientologists in the low thousands. Canada reported 1,745 members in the 2011 census. In the same year, Australia reported 2,163 members, a 13.7 percent decrease from the 2006 census number.[7] Scientology's United Kingdom public affairs director claimed the United Kingdom had 118,000 members, 15,000 of them being "active members" in 2013.[8] The 2001 census in England and Wales identified 1,781 Scientologists.[9]

At visitors' centers around the world, Scientologists use exhibits and videos to share their religious beliefs with potential converts.

States. Since the time of its founding by L. Ron Hubbard more than half a century ago, Scientology has undergone many transformations. Today, Scientologists seek to continue spreading their beliefs and practices across the world.

ESSENTIAL FACTS

DATE FOUNDED

L. Ron Hubbard established the Church of Scientology in 1954.

BASIC BELIEFS

Scientology centers on the notion that humans are spiritual beings called thetans. The thetan is immortal. It has lived for many lifetimes and will continue to live after the body dies. The thetan uses the mind and body it occupies. Dianetics is a process that allows an individual to remove destructive images, or engrams, from the subconscious mind that may create physical or mental impairment. A person who has removed all engrams is called Clear. Once Clear, people can move on as Operating Thetans (OTs) to discover and enhance their spiritual nature. People can improve their lives and develop their full potential by using the technology of auditing developed by L. Ron Hubbard.

IMPORTANT HOLIDAYS AND EVENTS

- March 13 (birthday of L. Ron Hubbard)
- May 9 (first publication of *Dianetics*)
- June 6 (first voyage of the *Freewinds*)
- Auditor's Day (second Sunday in September)

FAITH LEADERS

⊙ L. Ron Hubbard was the founder of Scientology; his writings and lectures are the source for all Scientology doctrine.

⊙ David Miscavige has been the head of Scientology as director of the Religious Technology Center since 1987.

NUMBER OF PEOPLE WHO PRACTICE SCIENTOLOGY

The Church of Scientology claims approximately 10 million members. Other sources, including Scientology dissenters, ex-members, and government organizations, estimate approximately 30,000 to 50,000 members worldwide.

QUOTE

"Nothing in Scientology is true for you unless you have observed it and it is true according to your observation."

—L. Ron Hubbard

GLOSSARY

ALLEGATION
A claim or assertion.

CHARISMATIC
Having charm that inspires devotion in others.

DEFAMATION
The act of damaging someone's reputation through false statements.

DOCTRINE
What is taught; teachings.

ENTREPRENEUR
A person who organizes and operates a business or businesses.

IN ABSENTIA
Without being present.

INDICT
To formally accuse someone of a crime.

INSULAR
Ignorant or not interested in things outside one's own culture.

LIBEL
A published false statement that is damaging to a person's reputation.

NEUROSIS
A relatively mild mental illness without a physical cause.

PULP FICTION
Fictional stories and books created in large quantities with low quality.

SHUN
To avoid, ignore, and reject someone.

TRAUMATIC
Emotionally disturbing or distressing.

UNINDICTED COCONSPIRATOR
Someone who is named in an indictment but is not charged.

ADDITIONAL RESOURCES

SELECTED BIBLIOGRAPHY

Lewis, James R., ed. *Scientology*. New York: Oxford UP, 2009. Print.

Wright, Lawrence. *Going Clear: Scientology, Hollywood, and the Prison of Belief*. New York: Vintage, 2013. Print.

FURTHER READINGS

Melton, J. Gordon. *The Church of Scientology*. Salt Lake City, UT: Signature Books, 2000. Print.

Urban, Hugh. *The Church of Scientology: The History of a New Religion*. Princeton, NJ: Princeton UP, 2011. Print.

ONLINE RESOURCES

To learn more about Scientology, visit **abdobooklinks.com**. These links are routinely monitored and updated to provide the most current information available.

MORE INFORMATION

For more information on this subject, contact or visit the following organizations:

CHURCH OF SCIENTOLOGY
scientology.org

The website of the Church of Scientology features information about the church, its beliefs, and its practices.

WORLD RELIGIONS & SPIRITUALITY PROJECT
wrldrels.org

Created by Virginia Commonwealth University, the World Religions & Spirituality Project aims to provide reliable, objective information about the world's religions, including Scientology.

SOURCE NOTES

Chapter 1. Going Clear

1. Adam Boult. "My Scientology Personality Test." *Guardian*. Guardian, 29 Sept. 2010. Web. 10 Apr. 2018.

2. Tony Ortega. "Prepare to Be Audited: Claire Headley Takes Us through Scientology's 'ARC Straightwire.'" *Underground Bunker*. Underground Bunker, 7 Aug. 2013. Web. 10 Apr. 2018.

3. "Michael Peña." *Celebrity Centre International*. Church of Scientology, 2018. Web. 10 Apr. 2018.

4. "Michael Peña: Scientology 'Made Me a Better Actor.'" *US Magazine*. US Magazine, 6 Oct. 2016. Web. 10 Apr. 2018.

Chapter 2. L. Ron Hubbard and Dianetics

1. "An Introduction to L. Ron Hubbard." *L. Ron Hubbard*. Church of Scientology, n.d. Web. 10 Apr. 2018.

2. "An Introduction to L. Ron Hubbard."

3. Lawrence Wright. *Going Clear: Scientology, Hollywood, and the Prison of Belief*. New York: Vintage, 2013. Print. 35.

4. Hugh B. Urban. *The Church of Scientology: A History of a New Religion*. Princeton, NJ: Princeton UP, 2011. Print. 52.

Chapter 3. From Science to Religion

1. Hugh B. Urban. *The Church of Scientology: A History of a New Religion*. Princeton, NJ: Princeton UP, 2011. Print. 53.

2. Janet Reitman. *Inside Scientology: The Story of America's Most Secretive Religion*. New York: Houghton Mifflin Harcourt, 2011. Print. 30.

3. Reitman, *Inside Scientology*, 26.

4. Reitman, *Inside Scientology*, 26.

5. Urban, *The Church of Scientology*, 38.

6. Reitman, *Inside Scientology*, 85.

7. Reitman, *Inside Scientology*, 38.

8. "Most Published Works by One Author." *Guinness World Records*. Guinness World Records, 2006. Web. 10 Apr. 2018.

9. Reitman, *Inside Scientology*, 45.

Chapter 4. Growth and Expansion

1. Hugh B. Urban. *The Church of Scientology: A History of a New Religion*. Princeton, NJ: Princeton UP, 2011. Print. 67.

2. Janet Reitman. *Inside Scientology: The Story of America's Most Secretive Religion*. New York: Houghton Mifflin Harcourt, 2011. Print. 51.

3. Donald A. Westbrook. "Walking in Ron's Footsteps: 'Pilgrimage' Sites of the Church of Scientology." *Numen: International Review for the History of Religions* 63.1 (2016): 71–94.

4. Donald A. Westbrook. "Saint Hill and the Development of Systematic Theology in the Church of Scientology (1959–1967)." *Alternative Spirituality and Religion Review* 6.1 (2015): 116.

5. Westbrook, "Saint Hill," 150.

Chapter 5. Afloat

1. Romeo Vitelli. "Implanting False Memories." *Psychology Today*. Psychology Today, 4 Nov. 2012. Web. 10 Apr. 2018.

SOURCE NOTES CONTINUED

Chapter 6. Landfall

1. Lawrence Wright. *Going Clear: Scientology, Hollywood, and the Prison of Belief.* New York: Vintage, 2013. Print. 122.

2. Janet Reitman. *Inside Scientology: The Story of America's Most Secretive Religion.* New York: Houghton Mifflin Harcourt, 2011. Print. 123.

3. Roger Ebert. "Battlefield Earth." *RogerEbert.com.* Roger Ebert, 12 May 2000. Web. 10 Apr. 2018.

Chapter 7. Restructuring the Church

1. Janet Reitman. *Inside Scientology: The Story of America's Most Secretive Religion.* New York: Houghton Mifflin Harcourt, 2011. Print. 169.

2. Rachel Browne. "What 'Going Clear' Means for the Decline of Scientology." *Maclean's.* Maclean's, 8 May 2015. Web. 10 Apr. 2018.

3. "Way to Happiness." *Scientology.* Church of Scientology, n.d. Web. 10 Apr. 2018.

4. "The Truth about Drugs." *Scientology.* Church of Scientology, n.d. Web. 10 Apr. 2018.

5. Tess Maune. "5 More Lawsuits Filed Against Narconon Arrowhead Rehab Facility." *News on 6.* News on 6, 21 Mar. 2013. Web. 10 Apr. 2018.

6. "An Introduction to Criminon." *Scientology.* Church of Scientology, n.d. Web. 10 Apr. 2018.

Chapter 8. Celebrities and Controversies

1. Troy Patterson. "Tom Cruise on Tom Cruise, Scientologist." *Slate*. Slate, 17 Jan. 2008. Web. 10 Apr. 2018.

Chapter 9. The Future of Scientology

1. "Scientology—A World Religion." *Freedom Magazine*. Church of Scientology, n.d. Web. 10 Apr. 2018.

2. Ned Zeman. "Scientology's Vanished Queen." *Vanity Fair*. Vanity Fair, Mar. 2014. Web. 10 Apr. 2018.

3. "The Global Religious Landscape: Jews." *Pew Research Center*. Pew Research Center, 18 Dec. 2012. Web. 10 Apr. 2018.

4. Mike Rinder. "10 Million Scientologists—Where Are They?" *Something Can Be Done about It*. Mike Rinder, 9 Nov. 2014. Web. 10 Apr. 2018.

5. "Have You Ever Wondered How Many Scientologists There Really Are?" *Dangerous Minds*. Dangerous Minds, 17 July 2014. Web. 10 Apr. 2018.

6. "Motor Vessel *Freewinds*." *Scientology*. Church of Scientology, n.d. Web. 10 Apr. 2018.

7. Steve Cannane. "Census Shows Scientology Numbers Going Backwards." *ABC*. ABC News, n.d. Web. 10 Apr. 2018.

8. Jonathan Brown. "Scientologists Plan £6m 'Country Estate' Headquarters in Birmingham." *Independent*. Independent, 15 Mar. 2013. Web. 10 Apr. 2018.

9. "How Many Members Do They Really Have?" *Church Times*. Church Times, 29 Nov. 2006. Web. 10 Apr. 2018.

INDEX

ABOUT THE AUTHOR

Cynthia Kennedy Henzel has a BS in social studies education and an MS in geography. She has worked as a teacher-educator in many countries. Currently, she works writing books and developing education materials for social studies, history, science, and ELL students. She has written more than 80 books for young people.